PRAISE FOR *Poems from the Fields of Dharma* . . .

"Thomas's poetry gives real meaning to Teilhard de Chardin's now ubiquitous observation: 'We are not human beings having a spiritual experience. We are spiritual beings having a human experience.' As we do the work of seeing spiritual meaning in our human experience, these poems are a loving hand offered to us fellow travelers."

—J. HAVENS, HEALTH DATA ANALYST (RET)

"This work reflects a lifetime of introspection and spiritual observation by a man willing to listen and be vulnerable to the tugs of the heart, the whispering of the spirit, and the directives of his soul."

—RUDY ANDERSON, EARLY CHILDHOOD SPECIALIST

"Thomas's poems are a rich, love-woven tapestry of his personal journey in the discovery of soul. Sit back, relax, and enjoy the beauty that is to be unveiled!"

—DEBRA KUSZEWSKI, LICENSED MASSAGE THERAPIST

"*Poems from the Fields of Dharma* inspires us to look beyond our worldly concerns in order to experience the great mysteries that lie within. Each poem makes spirit's presence more palpable and invites soulful contemplations that enhance self-reflection."

—JAMIE PITTS, COFOUNDER OF GREATAUPAIR

"The reader joins the poet's soulful journey from the mundane to the spiritual. Reminiscent of Rumi, he radiates self-awareness, love, gratitude, and acceptance as he communes with the divine."

—KATHY HOWARTH
TEACHER, ENGLISH AS A SECOND LANGUAGE, US AND JAPAN

"Noël Hudson's small collages are meditations.... The variety of materials themselves force a meeting and resolution of Eastern and Western sensibilities."

—KATHLEEN SLOAN
ARTS WRITER

"Hudson's [collages] are beautifully edited glimpses, embodied moments, flashes of memory, time, place, and sensory perception. They are intense yet delicate; expansive yet contained; grand yet small. These truly are ... gems."

—CYNTHIA SÁNCHEZ, PhD
DIRECTOR, CAPITOL ART FOUNDATION
CURATOR, CAPITOL ART COLLECTION

Poems from The Fields of Dharma

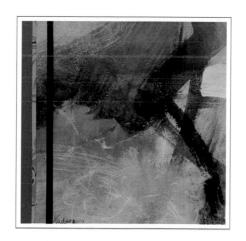

Thomas Reidy

Art by Noël Hudson

To Nancy and Haines —
Thomas
Noël

B·L·U·E
SPRUCE
BOOKS

Santa Fe, New Mexico

Published by

BLUE SPRUCE BOOKS

7 Avenida Vista Grande, Suite B7 #208

Santa Fe, New Mexico 87508

bluesprucebooks.com

Editors: Leslie S. King and Ellen Kleiner
Book design and production: Angela Werneke

First Edition

Text copyright © 2015 by Thomas Reidy
Images copyright © 2015 by Noël Hudson

Printed in Korea

PUBLISHER'S CATALOGING–IN-PUBLICATION

Reidy, Thomas.
    Poems from the fields of dharma / Thomas Reidy ; art by Noël
    Hudson. – First edition. – Santa Fe, New Mexico : Blue Spruce
    Books, [2015]

        pages : illustrations ; cm.

        ISBN: 978-0-9908063-0-1 (pbk.) ; 978-0-9908063-1-8
    (ebook)
        Summary: A poetic journal that chronologically details the
    forty-year awakening the author discovered after years of
    battling inner conflict and strife. The subject matter of the
    poems ranges from recollections of lives lived long ago to
    Reidy's inner surrender to love and truth. The subtly evocative
    poems in combination with seven full-color works of art
    penetrate the soul to awaken something within: knowledge,
    power, or desire.—Publisher.

        1. Spiritual life—Poetry. 2. Spiritual biography—Poetry.
    3. Dharma—Poetry. 4. Sufi poetry. 5. Consciousness—Poetry.
    6. Spirituality—Poetry. 7. Love—Poetry. 8. Truth—Poetry.
    9. Soul—Poetry. 10. Spirit—Poetry. 11. Inspiration—Poetry.
    12. American poetry. 13. Art, Abstract. I. Hudson, Noël, 1943–
    II. Title.

PS3618.E5528 P64 2015   2014916216
811/.6—dc23   1411

1 3 5 7 9 10 8 6 4 2

To Sri Gary Olsen

Acknowledgments

For help in bringing this book into the world, I thank Noël Hudson, Lesley S. King, Ellen Kleiner, Angela Werneke, and, for the inspiration, Rumi, Hafiz, Kabir, and other Sufi mystic poets.

CONTENTS

III. Love Songs

IV. The Universe of Soul

V. The Art of Devotion

VI. Nothing, Nothing but the Master

VII. A Moment in Eternity

LIST OF ILLUSTRATIONS

INTRODUCTION
Stepping-Stones into the Garden of Love

Some fifty years ago in a forest cabin nestled in the California redwoods I heard a silent voice say to me, "You are not your thoughts," a message that marked the beginning of my quest for understanding the meaning of intuition and true identity. This book is a poetic diary of my expanding consciousness and my inner surrender to the love and the truth of the masters in order to comprehend these notions. It originated during a childhood of early challenges, joys, and traumas, as many have experienced. As a young man, I was closed off, unwilling to accept the life I was dealt and rebelling against everything. Not until I began to truly listen to the unsolicited inner promptings did my anger start to dissolve.

I experienced my first major intuition as a teenager. After graduating from high school, two friends and I took the family car to Glacier Point in Yosemite National Park. We were holding on to the railing as we stood 3,200 feet above the canyon floor watching a beautiful storm developing across the valley when suddenly I received an inner message saying, "Step back from the rail." We took a couple of steps back, and instantly lightning struck the rail, turning the world electric with ozone and yellow light. We ran away from the cliff edge, shaken but elated at the near miss. I have periodically received many such messages following that incident, and the poems in this book flow from the same source as that warning I received as a teenager.

In the many years since then, I have married and had a family; spent time in the US Army in Austria, where I began to explore architecture; divorced; "dropped out"; delivered a child; and taken a hundred acid trips as the beginning part of my journey of discovery. But it was not until I picked up a book that spoke about saints, gurus, and spiritual paths that I recognized—in a revelation similar to that flash before a lightning strike—what my purpose was in this incarnation. After that I studied with a Tibetan Buddhist teacher, and then an Apache medicine woman. Many wild experiences occurred during those years as I kept searching to find the self with which I was comfortable—my true self.

Eventually my journey brought me to New Mexico, where I continued my fifty-year career as a carpenter, builder, and architect, six of which involved designing housing, health facilities, and commercial buildings for the Navajo and Pueblo peoples. This period provided an opening to acceptance of the diversity of humankind.

My experience with Native Americans coincided with the beginning of my journey with my spiritual teacher, Sri Gary Olsen, which changed everything. All my prior seeking ended; I had found what I had been searching for. One day he answered two questions: "Have I been with you before?" and "Have you been with me this whole life?" When he answered yes to both questions, I knew that everything is the path.

This book is an attempt to illustrate that point. It contains poems written over forty years, starting some years before I re-united in this life with Sri Gary. The early poems seem to be about remembering prior lifetimes on this path, while they all reflect my expansion in consciousness and my inner surren-der to love and truth. Collectively, they are stepping-stones into the garden of love. My process of writing them is that I get a title and then the rest of the poem flows to me while I simply record it. The poems, which help to quiet my mind and emo-tions, show me love and acceptance for what is and what is be-coming my experience. The experience is an opening pushing aside everything else in my being, including all thoughts. I be-come empty with the acceptance of everything as it is in its perfection. This is a directive to let the universe unfold as it will, without criticism, without wanting to change it, without wanting to jump in and do something. Just being myself is enough.

Yet my experience with this is not complete. While overall I live within a very beautiful peace, every once in a while my anger returns and I forget to relax my mind and emotions. That is when I remember the path and the ongoing task of surrender-ing to the inner choice of love over the small self.

My life today offers a continual teaching. I reside in a quiet home, which my wife, Noël Hudson, and I built in Santa Fe, New Mexico. I'm fortunate to have the companionship of my wife on the path, and many of the poems are about our forty-year journey together. Because of this dynamic relationship, I can't get away with anything. It's challenging and loving. Noël is an artist, and a number of her collages illuminate this book.

Perhaps the word that most defines this journey is *surrender*—surrender of the mind's programming to that quiet inner voice that knows everything and guides me to my true self. Just as Rumi attributed his understandings to his master, Shams of Tabriz, and Hafiz cited his master, Attar, I honor mine in the poems, simply calling him "master" or by the name of his inner form, "Garji," recognizing that the inner *sat* (true) *guru*—soul, or true self—is the ultimate master and that everything I do is from the *sat guru*, facilitated by my outer master, who is the perfect teacher and earthly representative of the *sat guru*.

It is my true self that I am increasingly becoming. This inner path is the called *surat shabda yoga*, the practice of merging soul with spirit. Shabda is the universal soul, or consciousness. It is the sound current, the Divine-into-expression power, what has been termed "the Word," "the Tao," or "the Holy Spirit." When I am quiet and attentive, this current directs all my thoughts, words, and actions. Many Sufi mystic poets of the past called this Divine energy, as embodied by living masters, "the friend" to circumvent the religious intolerance of their times.

Over the years I have become enlivened, guided, loved, and nourished by this silence, which speaks my truth. May these poems help the reader relax and feel the love and joy I have been graced to know.

1

PERPETUALLY SEEKING

His heart will teach him
everything he thinks he now knows.

TWO WORLDS

Migrant Worker in the Fields of Dharma

Dirty
sweat-soaked traveler,
a tiller of soul.
Harvester of patterns embedded
into the mind of long ago.
To consider:
access and choose the impulse
that stirs something beyond this worker,
something that is sensed at first
then known as only the soul knows
patterns from lives lived and forgotten.
Dialogues within, irrigating emotions,
attempt clarity above all else and
struggle across the borders of consciousness
perpetually seeking the El Norte of light.

1986

Ron

With his intellect burning like the hot coals of a fire walker,
he seeks to understand his path.
He treads quickly over the panorama of his work,
moving like the mistral wind from aspect to aspect.
He flashes wit and tongue
as a swordsman before an adversary,
forgetting that such posturing reveals
the uncertainty of self.
He is strong.
His depth lies rooted within his soul
which he can reach only through the stillness of a mind
now restless.
He will triumph
for it is through the unbearable pain in his being
that he will learn love.
His heart will teach him everything he thinks he now knows.

1986

BREATH

Out of the vibrant stillness
the winds of life come forth
to fill the spaces within each.
Unseen, perhaps—
not unfelt—
they magnetize that which is still,
charging every particle with movement
and so
create the universe of the atom
the eye
and the soul.

1987

The Pushing

So long have I heard this voice
of my ancient sorrow.
So long has my discontent drowned me,
clouding my understanding in illusion and ignorance.
Why then this suffering—
this struggle to master my turmoil
and live for the day to unravel itself?
Why can I not understand its cause?
Is my illusion my sorrow?
Is my ignorance the root of my sadness?
And why then
so much self-concern?

1990

GRACE

Blessings are the commitments of help
from realms of spirit.
Gratitude brings forth that which we
need for growth.
Can there be one
without the other?

1990

Awakening

I have promised my soul to love
giving up the struggle of the "I"
to bequeath itself an inheritance of pain.
Years of escape and lifetimes of diversion are the power
behind the promise.
The dull ache of emptiness falls
back into the abyss—spiraling across the memory,
creating compassion and gratitude as it shapes events
in all directions.
"When" does not matter, for "when" never existed
except before the promise.
"I" always existed—it is the promise;
and "when" was the pain.

1990

Heaven Dreams

Heaven dreams
of a life of harmony
given to the daydreams of mortals.
Mortals dream
of a life in heaven,
forsaking the truth
of the days of living.

1990

Winter Dust

On the eve of winter
I am bombarded by the myth of brotherhood.
Empty eyes reach out, revealing but a spark of the soul,
carrying the longing and pain
that is rooted in their illusion of self.
The imperative of the season brings the images of communion
to an empty crowd,
giving us a glimpse of possibilities.
I want to know you.
I want to know you without struggling to overcome
the constructions of our lives behind us.
Let go of the self you imagine to be you, and talk to me
from your heart of soul.
I will walk with you
for I have fallen often enough to know that my perfect self
is dust.

1990

SOUL

What of the light?

Is it born of life itself?

Or is it earned like merits at a summer camp?

I should think the light is with us from

the unknowable beginning, when we,

scattered as stardust, first gathered together.

Antares, Pleiades, and Sirius—

home?

Home to portions of us we haven't a clue about

save those intuitive rumblings constantly moving within us

as we abide in this denseness.

Light! Pray you peel away those gross coverings of matter

that I may see you once again whole.

You come disguised now,

given that my eyes see so little.

Or is it really my eyes?

1990

Coda
Code

Hope:
Aboriginal dreamtime is a seed of harmony
planted in the true self of seekers.
Forged out of the nobility of destiny,
they focus rays of compassion
upon dead dreams of glory.
Prayer pipe, contemplation,
sweat lodge, and silence cleanse the soul, body, and mind,
loosening the grip of the need for triumph.
The mastery gained then
is of ourselves.

1990

CODE
CODA

The warriors of the planet
have bonded themselves
to a code toxic to their souls.
Cycles of energy they cannot control
propel them toward each other
with arms raised in dread and anguish.
There are no innocents,
for fear created this code—
fear born in the separation of self.
Corporate madness concocts kings,
soldiers, politicians, and the homeless.
Survival rules the city.
Citizens and workers alike seek escape in crystals,
philanthropy, art, money, or drugs,
forever wondering if times will change.
Not the warrior,
for conflict is the law.
Prayers to the master
that we be released.

1991

High Step

Whence comes the counsel?
Master of stewardship,
grant me the wisdom to know your voice
amid the rumblings of discontent.
Let me discard
the gift of protection
that is no longer needed,
the armor of the child
donned by fear of loneliness and abandonment.
Let me embrace that child.
Let me hold him tight in arms of forgiveness,
giving him a life at peace with himself.
Let me hold the staff of abundance firmly,
hand in hand with that child of long ago.
I shall step gracefully over the corpse of my rage.

1991

Midnight Rain

I am as hollow as the reed
with whispers of dread flowing through my heart.
The emptiness I feel is pregnant with a paralysis of fear.
Longings reborn course their way over the devastation
of the last few days
where masks of expectations
lay crushed under the onslaught of truth.
Midnight rain soothes the earth and carries my dreams
into the river of solitude.
Hush, I can speak my heart here.

1992

POWER

Not your average white man's
energies in motion.
Producer of change through
ideas in manifestation.
Magnetic.
Electric.
One's sense of self
becomes one's awareness
of the truth of the universe.
Flexible, like the river grass,
clarity of presence
creates the ability to recognize
and include,
and the gift to cooperate without fear.
Wisdom begets
compassion.
Love becomes power,
and power surrenders to truth.

1993

Conspiracy of Mediocrity

Impounded by forms and ideas of the past
the citizens struggle to maintain that which is.
Acceptance of the known
is enforced at every turn.
Intuition withers;
information rules.
Creativity,
the flight of the river heron,
the track of the saint and shaman—
all maneuver to stay above the mud of the norm.
The painter of impressions
applies the colors of emotions
to show us what could be
and the planet moves unceasingly toward the referendum of
grace.
The seekers know that anything is possible.
Citizens resent the change.
Isn't that inevitable?

1993

Rude Attitude

Here's the deal:
Commenting on life
as it appears to you
changes the experience for everyone;
observing the same events
in sacred silence
changes only yourself.
If you can live with the consequent responsibility,
say what you want.

1996

Noël

What can I reveal to you
that will ignite that spark of curiosity
to ask about who you are?
Or am I being too vain
in thinking this would indeed help you?
Your pain is your guide and savior now.
Perhaps your fear is more truthful than anything
I can say to you.
Yet, I want to show you so much
about how we are
in the truth as I live it.
Soul, which has a mind?
Soul, which has emotions?
Soul, which has karma?
Soul that we surrender to
in order to rise above all else
in this material world.
Soul, which is love.

2004

II
COVERINGS AND REFLECTIONS

The illusion of the physical, emotional, and mental realms
is a trap we fall into,
missing the eternal beauty of soul.

VEIL OF MYSTERY

SILHOUETTES

Winter—
dusty gray cottonwoods frame the silver sky.
Powder snow falls.

1987

Yuppie Dharma

Going for the gold,
the worker labors twenty years in his schoolyard.
Information fills each moment,
allowing no peace,
no quiet.
Stretching as far as the imaginings,
there is only striving and gathering.
No time for reflecting on the still light upon the crow's wing
that turns the black to silver.

1990

CHILDREN IN ASHES

The children,
afraid,
they gather here,
surrounded by the dust of their ancestors' greed,
mourning the loss of innocence.
Fires of confusion and rage burn deep
within their being,
the rage, fanned by the seeming impotence of youth,
not yet hopeful of change.
Change—a demand for the honesty
lost when we first stepped out of harmony
with our birthright.
A legacy of ashes bequeathed to the children
honors naught but the fears of the fathers.
Is it any wonder the children don't listen to you?
What can you tell them?

1991

ANOTHER LOOK

What is it that I can no longer see?
Reading about the plight of men
at the end of this century
calls to question origins and endings unknown.
I thought there was just the process
of becoming our true selves.
Perhaps there is more.
Angels of destruction,
myth-slayers, waiting out our days,
casting our sons into the furnace of denial.
Keepers of the flame of misogyny,
we push our women to the point of extinction,
thereby ensuring our own.
Perhaps there is more.
I see soft hope in the music and poets
carving a pathway through the clamor of opinions
brought to us by the languages of long ago.
Would it help to burn the books and start again?
How else to capture memories of the soul,
unwashed by the beliefs of people around us?
Clear then, within the margins of our being,
we could once again be whole.

1991

Taos Ninety-One

Timeless landscape
filled with empty promises
of racial harmony.
Bitterness and suspicion abound.
Scarred by the struggle of remoteness
and indifference to values,
the workers heave mightily into the winds of progress,
hoping to harvest a living from the bones of the land.
Unaware of the spirit lodge
built by the devotion of angels,
local man has set before himself
a feast of dead ideals.
Profit at any cost becomes the password
into the playhouse of the connected.
Prayerful vigils give solace
to the out-of-time hippie
and the ecofreaks of no growth.
Politicians push,
and developers anguish in the delay of earnings.
The hearse of time rumbles by,
carrying within
the corpse of the acequias and the vegas land.

We hear the drumroll of mourning played for all it's worth
by immigrants and peddlers of T-shirts,
firewood, *ristras*, and houses.
The revered painters of landscapes and totems
pollute the very air and soil they profess to worship
by the toxic substances used for their canvases of illusion.
Galleries of dreamers in the doorways of sales rooms
invoke the mighty collector.
Runways and malls steal the headlines
from schools in limbo, wars, and banks in dissolution.
What then of the land, the mountain, and the river?
What change there from the spirit?
Have they the grace to survive,
and will we recognize their distress in time?

1991

Millennia

The Lords of the Material Essence
seduced us with their touch,
and our senses ruled.
We wrapped ourselves
in worlds of form and danced,
delighted in the lights
and sounds of this creation.
Songs of angels became words.
Words became language.
We believed in the terms
and forgot who we were.
Awakened from the tyranny
of our voices
we become whole again.
Trusting in our heart's intelligence
we no longer overlook
ourselves.

1992

Colors

I know:
I am a man
I am "white"
my skin is white
my mind is white.
I know not the color of my soul.
I am not deceived by this mind,
which tells me what and that.
Instead, I listen intently
to the silence
beyond the heart's beating
and the thoughts to and fro
for direction from the
innermost master,
my true self.
Sixty years of labor within this form
have given me the grace, when I am quiet,
to put aside appearances
and look upon the world
as a place to greet in the morning
with a simple hello.

1994

THE ANCHOR

Soul is the true seeker
in the ocean of love and mercy.
Mind is the sea anchor
filled with the tides of karma.
The master changes the anchor
to a sieve.

2002

THE REFLECTION

Is the image in the mirror important?
A little, perhaps.
More important
than the wonder of the body
is the unseen reflection
of the master—the *shabda*—
projected onto the world
in my actions and attitude.
The *shabda* manifests through me
so that I take more care
with the balance and harmony within
than I do with the
image in the mirror.

2005

SEEING

Most of my seeing
is an illusion
because I see with only two things:
my eyes
and my mind.
Objects appear to be real
as my eyes or mind sees them.
Soul, however, sees the spaces
between things.

2009

Coverings

How many layers surround me?
Physical.
Emotional.
Mental.
The realms of cause and effect.
This body is but a cage,
necessary in the search for truth,
and a distraction at best,
as are emotions and the mind,
absorbed, as they are, in impermanent stuff.
The illusion of the physical, emotional, and mental realms
is a trap we fall into, missing the eternal beauty
of soul.
We return to these coverings
countless times
until we transcend
their limitations and morph
into our true selves.

2011

WINDOW SINK

Hands warm
with hot soapy water
I look up to find
an intense blue sky
beyond the
crystalline powder snow
blowing off
the trees
and roof
reminding me
of the nature
of thoughts
plans
and emotions
without guidance
from the friend.

2013

We Come

We come,
appearing out of nowhere
our minds can conceive of.
Looking around,
we find a seemingly solid
world
teeming with all kinds of
noise,
objects,
illusions,
and ghosts
of forgotten lives.
Here there's a silence
that opens the
world of truth to us,
if we would only
stop looking
around
with our eyes
and thoughts.

2013

III
LOVE SONGS

Without guile or expectation of heroism
you hold me close to you and I sense a voyage of time shared
beyond these pitiful limitations of physical life.

DRAPED IN RED SILK

TWENTY-ONE JUNE

Solstice:
In the beginning
of a new life
we arrange this space
which has become our apartment.
Scared,
and elated,
we stand with the choices
born of our dreams of sharing this life
with one another.
Solstice:
This longest of days
marks the beginning
of the most fruitful
time of the year.

1975

Discovery

Blessings through the telephone in my hand.
Unspoken thoughts dance around us
uniting in the auric energy
like magic
from the Lords of Time and Destiny.
Caution cautions,
for distance enchants the ignoble lust
into a higher action and creates a pathway
for me to express my love
with pen and word.
Draw for her
the essence of love in verse.
Reach out beyond the earthbound
illusion toward that holiest of unions.
Say, "I love you."
Say it and erase the fears,
for to have found someone to love
is indeed a great blessing.

1975

Hands On

Hearty appetites for touching
propel us to the white
coverlet.
A brush of the hand
stirs a rustle of thoughts.
But why ask?

1977

VOYAGE

Sincerely beloved,
at last I am beginning to understand
the sweetness of your love.
Without guile or expectation of heroism
you hold me close to you
and I sense a voyage of time shared
beyond these pitiful limitations
of physical life.
Thus, I abandon all my cherished
fantasies and sexual journeys
and reach out to you
from a depth of unwavering
devotion and commitment
to construct a life of understanding and growth
toward that highest ideal we share.
I exalt in my great fortune
and I ask forgiveness for my
transgressions of forgetfulness.
Like a naive child, I wander about
from experience to experience
until at last I am able to say, "I love you"
and know sincerely what that means.

1979

LAVENDER

Arms raised overhead
the lavender satin slides down
the back that is toward me.
With a slight tug
it is pulled over breasts
and down further
past hips it falls
covering and yet enhancing the body
with the change of light and texture.
It is like lake waters
illumined by the dusk.
To touch this lavender
is to invoke magic.

1985

THE KISS OF EROS

Salt/sweet licking
binds us together in the twilight.
Our caress in praise of Eros
arouses our appetites
to intermingle our bodies
and feelings.
Slowly/gently
this rhythm pulls us together,
slowly/deliberately
and with unhurried pulses we move,
spending the perfect moment
in joyful sensuality
blessed within this aura of love.

1986

GUILFORD

He sits in silence,
crowned by his duty,
this gray-bearded Zen bard,
apportioning his well-traveled wisdom of discipleship
from a rose-deep cave of long-sought solitude.
Reciting the life verse of the age,
he traces the footsteps of the seeker
through the land of emotion,
and filtering illusions of knowledge through
the stigmata of experience,
he creates a handhold on the ladder of aspiration.
With such grace has he abandoned
the raiments of the hierophant
and donned as his sackcloth the prayers of the beloved.
Given that he has danced a while
and that the seeds of his footsteps
have begun to harvest themselves,
he seeks to laugh at the postures
our fleeting images of personalities want to see
sculpted in stone.

Hands holding stones, black and white,
he reminds us of moderation
while living the virtues of brotherhood, face to face.
He sits there, having known me and been counsel
to the trials of the spirit and the thorns of the flesh—
making no judgment known, save when asked.
Crowned by his affection, this gray-bearded child of the son,
a brother, Guilford.

1986

BOUQUET

Do your eyes see
the spring
flowering in my heart?
I listen for footsteps
on the threshold of my passion.
Come,
there is a bouquet of time
waiting just inside.

1990

ANNIVERSARY FOURTEEN

I pause for a moment at the window.
Three crows catch my eye as I watch the sunset.
They are flying west,
silhouetted against a chrome yellow sky.
I have just cleaned house, picking up the magazines
and dusting a little.
I think of my beloved driving home in her green van.
How grateful I am to be here sharing what I can
at this time in our lives.
I trust that this season will fade
as other moments of struggle have passed before.
What I see is the great importance of faith, love, and history.
This is what I am here for, living life as it presents itself.
Loving as much as I can each moment,
each being, and each circumstance.
With the rock of our partnership as my guide,
nothing shall move me off my path.
My prayer is with the Medicine Lodge of Marriage.

1991

Genital Friction

Beyond the comfort and release
Beyond the paradigms media born
Beyond the hang-ups, guilt, and quirks
we bring to each other
our beings as offerings
on the altar of physicality.

Bonding beyond any that is known,
ties are created into lives
as yet unformed or unacknowledged.

Restraints upon freedom, perhaps,
or renewals of our unique pathways to union.
The answers are carried within records of the saints.

1991

Again

Escaping for the moment
all thoughts of the hereafter,
the world, or its migrations,
we touch, caress, and arouse in each other
the desire
to be at one with ourselves
in the now.
Images
pleasures
smells, secretions, and textures
urging and pushing
moving us around.
We respond beyond self,
into the joys and excitements
of beings in harmony.

1991

I Can Speak My Heart Here

Don't let my ready defenses take you by surprise.
They are but the confusion and doubt
surfacing once again.
There are times when the power is still with me,
or rather, still felt.
But this is a time of tears for dreams
once followed for naught and relationships lost
in the dust of ambitions.
I can ask forgiveness and carry that hope
into the coming days,
but I must forgive in the moment
choices that came with the energy of restriction—
unknown at the time and out of confusion, perhaps
but still with me, and still with you.
My greatest sorrow is your pain.
Yet day by day you try to help me see
what can be done to heal and rebuild.
I understand and am grateful.
Have faith in my love and my acceptance of the pain.

1992

Romantic?

Romance has for me
been a big part of past dreams and fantasies.
What of the romantic self?
I cannot pretend to know
what worth that self-realized being
who hovers just inside/outside my awareness
would place on my valentine.
It matters not to me though
for I have given from the heart.
To give is the essence of this spirit,
which guides me today.
The rest is just conjecture
as I reside in the wonder
of the gift that is you.

1995

Long Time Coming

Such a long time
to write a new love poem
to my beloved
in praise of our travels together
in this world of chaos and wonder.
Together
we have taken a step beyond
this sphere of illusion
into our own private creations,
where we seek to begin again in truth.
This is where we can merge into
the real sacred marriage
and where we can say, with meaning,
"Thank you, beloved,
you have helped make my path in this time
one of love and blessings."

2003

MIRACLE OF YEARS

Does it seem like
a long time?
Or does it seem like
only a lifetime ago
that we met and moved
to be together
on this path to
love?
The answer is
not so important
when we look
into the present
from the vantage point
of the experiences
we have shared.
That we are blessed
with this miracle
overwhelms me.
Blessings
to you, beloved.

2006

Thirty-Four Valentines

Come close,
closer,
deep inside where
we are true
to our selves.
Come close and watch
from that place
of peace and clarity
all that passes us by,
wanting to intrude
and confuse us.
Come close
to that union we search for
everywhere
outside with each other
inside with our selves.
Love them both
as each can show us the way.

2010

In Awe of You

You have blessed my life
far beyond
what words can reveal.
When thoughts of you
preside
a silent, innermost
feeling of joy
envelops all the spaces
inside this vessel
I call me.
You are the most wonderful
companion
I could have imagined.
You will become
the goddess
you seek.
You are
the goddess
of this sacred now.
You are
love and beauty.

2011

In the Year of Twelve

As you approach
the anniversary of your birth
you radiate
an immense beauty
that is both seen and unseen.
To those who observe
the surface of things
there is the woman of elegance,
beauty, and taste.
To the ones who,
by their nature,
are able to look beneath
the worlds of matter
there is that aura of love
that is at first felt by the emotions,
then heralded by the soul.
A true goddess
among us.
A blessing to all.

2012

An Anniversary Letter

My beloved:
Our togetherness
is sacred to me.
Beyond our trials and stresses
I feel a bond
of love toward you
that reaches farther
than I can
imagine.
I wake at night
beside you
and wonder at
my great good fortune
that I can reach
out and touch
my anchor
my lover
my muse
my companion
and my wife.
I am truly blessed.

2012

IV
THE UNIVERSE OF SOUL

I was the one
I was searching for.

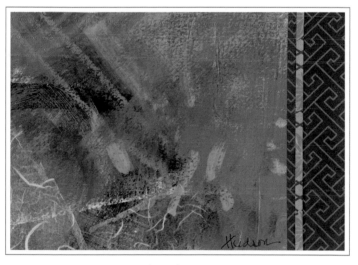

ASK ALICE

WHEEL

I
of my father
born of my mother's womb
a thousand times a thousand
to make peace
not with the world
but with myself.

1986

MIRROR OF LOVE

A kindness
given out of the stillness
of one's heart
has the qualities
of soul.
Refreshing as it touches
each in turn.
Like grace,
a clear reflection of polished light
spontaneous and uncluttered,
it shows us ourselves.

1990

THE DAWNING OF SOUL

As the sun rises over the rim of the world
so I, soul, rise over the edges of my mind
illuminating the universe of consciousness
in all directions.
Casting shadows where none have appeared before,
I walk through the desert of this dawning
feeling in those places of darkness
the roots of my behavior.
I am the warrior of spirit.
Armed with the blade of love,
I cut loose the vines of entrapments
grown out of lives long ago forgotten
in the mists of karma.
Looking into this morning of illumination,
I listen for the sweet voice of the master.
He is here with me, always guiding me
always reminding me that
yes,
I am.

1996

Soul

What of the sound?
It is life itself.
It is ours without work or merit for it is our very self.
If I should think about it I shall never find it
for it has always been before the "I."
We forgot who we were
and our obligations to spirit,
so we have come to this place to journey for a time
and gain the surrender necessary
to find our way home.
Blessed is the master,
for without his touch there is no home.

1999

Soul of My Longing

Sometimes,
when my attention is just so,
I can feel the weight
of my ignorance
and inexperience
like a sea anchor in the oceans of thought.
O Master.
O attention.
O soul.
Come to me, show me the way beyond
these mundane walls of my illusions,
and I will become my self.

1999

House Arrest

Detained in this body for centuries,
bound by the mind, emotions, and their effects,
I have come to the awareness that in order to escape
this narrow world
I must learn not to break out into more illusion
but to break in to the truth of soul,
the absolute master of life.
Unfettered by the myths of this universe
it soars in devout freedom homeward
toward its only goal.

1999

ILLUSIONS OF RIGHTEOUSNESS

Here
in our worlds of duality
yes
has no more value than
no.
Truth is
what the two have in common.

2002

A QUESTION

Do you know,
when *yes* is the answer,
who is replying,
and from
where this acceptance
begins?
Look beyond
what you admit.

2002

THIS MOMENT

This moment
when I am still,
I feel a great opening,
like the dawning
of morning light
moving through my being.
There is a deep yearning
to share this universe
of love
with all that is.
With the master's
blessing,
so shall it be.

2006

SHINING NOTHINGNESS

Blue skies.
The teeming blue oceans.
Rumbling radiant stones
giving up their magic
for our electronic toys.
Forests of creatures
on their way to extinction
with their canopies of green
becoming shelter for ourselves and
our children's children.
We dance and sing
about the relationships
we have missed
and join
in our search for the completion
we seek
while living in this
"shining nothingness"
built by the Divine.

2011

THE EMPTY

I can't try to be empty,
for
someone is here
to claim
its place,
filling up the
inner space
with the effort
to be absent.
All I can do
is be alone
with myself—
not wanting
anything else.
Quiet.
Aware.
Content.
In love.
Grateful.

2012

Looking

I always looked out
at beautiful objects
and ordinary things
to define myself
in this world.
I looked at what others had.
I looked at what I had,
judging,
comparing,
wanting
and rejecting.
I kept looking
until I found the path.
Then I relentlessly
searched everywhere
until I looked inside
and found that
I was the one I was searching for.

2012

The Call

From the sacred tower
of the inner master
the sound
goes within to my being.
"Come,
come,
come with me,"
it calls.
"Don't forget
why you are here
in this place.
Don't forget
to call within,"
it repeats.
I will hear you forever,
for
we are one.

2012

Even Me

The only thing
I can do
is be myself.
I will be guided
to myself
when I am quiet,
when I am loud,
when I am laughing,
when I am working.
Whenever I remember
to remember,
it is all *shabda*,
even me.

2012

Autumn Song

Yellow leaves
of thoughts
fall silently
into the
garden of soul.

2013

The Apprentice

Owning the gift of births
in form after form,
we apply our seemingly limitless
lifetimes of experience
to build upon and gain the ownership
of all thoughts, words, and deeds
fulfilling our apprenticeship
in the Divine's
Guild for the Masters.

2014

V

THE ART OF DEVOTION

Blessed One,

I am the grape you crushed

to make the wine of my soul.

AWAKENING

The Argument

It seems as though the spirit of romance
has left the temple
and confusion reigns.
It seems that the work is hard
and the joy has dimmed
in light of the struggle.
"Who will survive?"
is spoken to oneself.
Do we take apart what the spirit has joined?
Do we shy away from yet another task?
Do we love one another?
Beloved,
you are so of this life
that all I can do is surrender
to this love for you.
Else, I would be empty.

1977

A Poem

Yesterday
I promised my beloved
I would write her a poem.
I'm writing it today.
You see
we made love all yesterday.

1986

GIFT

I learn,
beloved,
by the art of surrender
for I cannot possess that which I seek.
It is not given to me
nor can I buy it anywhere.
You share it with all others
yet it is yours
and belongs to no one.
As I diminish
so does it grow
until, beloved,
I am not separate from any other
and I learn
that what I sought
was surrender itself.

1990

VALENTINE

I am amazed
dreaming of time spent together,
being as natural as the seasons.
Heartfelt tugs on my being
call to me
to grant all of the available wishes.
Like a visitor from far away
I encounter something new each hour
yet it is all grounded in the love
freely given
and freely accepted.

1992

Eighteen Years

Should anybody ask me about these years
I would say
they have been an extraordinary gift
founded in a dream and based on love and discovery.
They have been about movement,
change, and commitment.
Dedicated and faithful to that dream,
I was carried beyond ceremony and vows to a state of grace
exceeding all comprehension.
That dream, bringing images of the world to ease my pain
also delivered the gift of your presence,
your spirit, your beauty,
your endurance and perseverance.
My gift is this.

1994

LETTER TO THE MASTER

I can write a letter
to the master
at any time.
No pen,
paper, quill, or parchment
is used,
for it is written by the attention
and attitude
I hold
within every thought,
deed, and emotion.
Remember, Thomas,
it is read
in each moment
of eternity.

2005

WHAT YOU MEAN TO ME

Beloved,

you are my

muse

my companion

my friend

my guide

my critic

my collaborator

my mate

my helper

my wonder

my artist

my chef de cuisine

my wife

my lover

my partner

and

the most beautiful

woman in my life.

2006

WINE

Blessed One,
I am the grape
you crushed
to make the wine
of my soul.

2011

PAIN MANAGEMENT

The sharp, dull ache
of constant sciatic fever
takes my awareness from
the present
into some place I have never been before.
Contemplation brings a new clarity
into the root of this experience.
Accident?
Fall?
The art of building?
No.
The root is the Divine's
gift of healing
that which I have chosen to forget.
My soul rejoices
in the pain
wondering when will it be free
of the burden of
denial.

2011

The Apocalypse of Every Moment

This world dies
every moment we change
our attitude,
our understanding,
our thoughts.
Each time we change,
the world changes.
We rule the dying
and the rebirthing.
This world is within us—
not the other way around.
See the connection?
The apocalypse happens
with each change in our point of view.
Bless this moment of dying,
as it is our truth.

2011

WHAT WE SEE

We are the eyes of the creator.
What we see
the Divine sees.
Should we not
rest our eyes
on truth and beauty
to please our
friend?

2011

I Am My Prayer

There is no "thing"
I ask for.
I pray only
for the master's
love,
truth,
and beauty.

2012

INTERNET

I post thoughts
on the void
we call the web.
Hopefully they reflect
Simran . . .
Dhyan . . .
Bhajan . . .
If I am fortunate
and discriminating
they will be
sent in
love,
truth,
and beauty.

2012

Who's Telling?

What if I told you
that I rebelled against being told
what,
when,
how,
with whom,
or anything at all,
since I can remember.
What if I told you
that I was the one telling me
all of these things?
With the grace
of the master,
I recognize
the source
of this telling
and the rebellion
as me.
All along, the master
has been guiding
me to listen
to him.

2012

No Words

There is a feeling,
a knowing,
a being
that cannot be conveyed
by words
to express the nature
of my bond to you.
It is beyond speech,
beyond attachment,
beyond desire,
into the realms
of consciousness
that only our true self
can access and know.
This is the
deepest love I have known,
blessed by the
master.

2013

Writing Down the Silence

How do I write
of the quiet
stillness
I am given
by the blessings
of the friend?
It is a remembrance—
to remember him
in all actions
all thoughts
all words
and all deeds.
It is a joy
blooming within
this guy
called Thomas.

2013

INVITATION TO THE DANCE

How do we bend
like the grasses
in the currents
of streams
rivers and
wind?
By becoming flexible
in our thoughts,
actions,
attitudes,
and attention.
Love
is our dance.
Love
moves us
into the rhythms
colors
and
sound
of truth.

2013

Gospel of the Inner Master

The fragrant ark of a rose
welcoming my attention
in remembrance of the friend.
The quiet
within the constant din of life
around me.
Images of the dharma
like the newly mowed lawn
sequestered in the courtyard
with the leaves and grasses
on the compost pile.
Dishes washed
and put up.
Simple things
well done, without turning away
in frustration toward
a pleasure offered by
the other one who
lives within.
A constant
loving attitude given
to this path.

2014

The Consecration of Longing
(Santo Domingo de Oaxaca)

Gilded vaults
with jeweled figures
evoke saints and angels.
Stars and crosses and calligraphy abound
in remembrance of avatars and redeemers.
Figures carved in caves,
both miniature and giant;
forests of books
and universes of music;
preachers, pastors,
bishops, imams, and roshis—
all are present
to consecrate our longing for the
Divine.
Blessed are the *sat gurus*,
for they open inner doors
to the love, truth, and beauty
of our souls.

2014

VI
NOTHING, NOTHING
BUT THE MASTER

*The mind needs to fall in love with
something beyond itself.*

A MOMENT OF JOY

Coming Out

From within my solitude
I looked out and saw you
warm and affectionate
glowing with that certain intensity
that only a deep-knowing sensitivity can bring.
You touched me and I moved
not wanting to withdraw any longer
but dare I ask?
Can I tear open my heart
and speak of those forbidden images
crying to escape,
stifled for lack of a kindred soul?
They wait in their focused intensity,
for patience is mentor and guide
that leads me by the heart unerringly
to my last liberation
to love so completely as to offer
refuge from every action.
Will I leave my solitude?
Can I drink deep draughts
of that love shining in the eyes of the friend?
I take the first step and call out. Can you hear me?
I am the pilgrim.

1975

Father, This Time

Not having known you
longer than my first cycle of time,
I wonder at your absence still.
Perhaps as I look into what has become my past
I will find that which you are to me.
I grieved so long for you
that I thought
all the gods had left me standing alone
in the wilderness.
They did—
except for the one they named the master.
He is the initiator of discovery,
and given the chance,
he will find me beside the road
dusting off the ashes of life
with the golden feather of tears.

1991

GOOD LUCK

Years ago in darshan,
when the master said,
"Good luck at trying to contain the *shabda*,"
I did not know what he meant.
Now, after reading Kabir
and of the arrow
the master shot into his heart,
am I beginning to understand
the great good fortune
of the thousand deaths at the hand
of the master.

1998

I Dreamt I Was Weeping

You were gone
and I was weeping.
Like a lover who has vanished
you had left me
to suffer the pains of separation.
"What of me?" I asked,
oblivious of the obvious.
I had made choices that
pushed you into the background
of my attention.
Now I begin to see
I can never let my attention
wander so far from you that you
disappear
from my awareness
ever again.
This hurts too much
and makes me doubt
my very existence.
For I am you
and you are me.

2003

Remembrance

These days are different
these days of waking into a new energy
built within by the master.
It comes as I ask for it
through my remembrance
of him.
Simran.

2003

Pains of Separation

The soul is a happy, peaceful, and quiet entity.
The only reason we take drugs, drink alcohol,
or do anything in excess
is to ease the pain of separation from that state.
The way to return and remain in that state
without these diversions
is through the *sat guru*, *shabda*, and soul.
The way to begin this journey
is through the mind.
The tough part
is that the mind cannot
and will not
surrender to anything other
than something it loves
more than its own idea of self.
Therefore
the mind needs to fall in love with something
beyond itself.
Good morning, Garji.

2003

How Can I Tell?

Garji:
Of the many voices
I have heard over the years,
yours is the most loving and profound.
You are always direct,
to the point, and miraculously
accurate with guidance.
Even when I am off
on some tangent of my mind
or emotion, and have let my attention stray,
you are kind, patient, and
gentle with a reminder
of just who I need to be in the moment.

How can I tell?
I am much happier when
I remember you.

2004

VISION

Thirty years ago
in a loft by the sea
you appeared to me—
a figure before the window
for a moment,
then you were gone.
Yet you have remained
in my consciousness
ever since,
calling me home—
calling me to you,
Blessed One.
I am.

2009

Got No Right to Sing the Blues

I still love the blues.
But after the master held me
they had no place inside me to live.
Gone,
like the morning fog.
Burned away
by the sound.
They remind me
of where I've been,
not where I am.
I still love the blues.
They remind me
to sing my gratitude
and love—
not lost
but all around me.
I still love the blues.
They blessed me with
the master.

2011

On the Eve of Seventy-Eight

An opening up
creates a quiet inside
that has not been evident
in years.
Talking about the hollow
void inside
that had grown from childhood
changed it
to an acceptance of love
missing from so long ago
that it felt impossible to heal.
My words
grown out of the pains of separation
closed that wound
and opened my being
to the calm, healing joys
of love.
Much gratitude
to the master and my love.

2011

LOOK BEYOND

How big is the master?
I look beyond
the seminar,
the darshan,
and the teachings.
I look beyond my mind
and my struggles
to understand
what is not spoken
but is graced
with love and mercy.
In our entire incomprehensible
universe
there is nothing,
nothing
but the master.
Gratitude.

2012

The Trip
Some Divine Intervention

I
was going
down the drain,
and
I ended up
with the
master.

2012

Under Construction

Years ago,
without talking to the master
about our plans
for a new house
we had been designing
for the last several months,
we had darshan.
As I began to leave
this bliss,
the master
pointed to his
forehead and said,
"Build your house up here."
It is still under construction.

2012

HOMELESS

If we don't reside
with the Divine
we are homeless.

2012

Silence

Nothing is more eloquent
than
the silence of the beloved.

2013

STEPPING ASIDE

Walking into my contemplation
this morning,
the master spoke softly.
He said,
"All you have to do,
Thomas,
is step aside
and let me do
through you what
the Divine wants done."
So simple.
Rejoice in that relaxation
of habits and emotions.
Rejoice in the love
manifesting now.
Simply rejoice.

2014

VII
A Moment in Eternity

*Where can I be
but here in the now with you?*

INFINITE DISCOVERY

La Honda

On a soft and voluptuous earth side
approaching the sea,
cradling the redwoods
tall again after the great harvest of '06,
comes a majestic movement of creatures
embracing the contours of the hills.
Climbing up toward us,
looking as if a great Persian carpet had come to life,
thousands of vibrant winged butterflies appear.
Parting like we were rocks in a stream
they flow around us
as we sit for hours.
Entranced by the murmur of migration
we enter the great hall of silence.

1976

Sister

What a joy it is to watch your rebirth—
of woman and child unfolding,
of ancient archetypal power and wisdom
dancing in a maturing rhythm.
You will be the goddess.
You will burn with the mystic fires
of womb and breast.
Give forth only what you can bring to us.
Feminine to the bone,
do not fear your strength
for you have given birth to worlds and stars
without number.

1978

NIGHT SHIFT

Dense
overlays of dreamwork
lap into the day after.
It is as if you labored all night.
Perhaps you were in some realm
where conflict resolution
takes on different realities.
Truths—
mundane, esoteric and ritualistic—
are pulled from the far distant pathways
walked when the worker was younger.
As time becomes kaleidoscopic
the consequential things come first.

1991

Time Gone to Ninety-Two

Spring
of the leap year.
I have been tending
the gardens of our house in the city,
little by little
discovering plantings
placed by another,
delighting in the blooms just beginning.
Unfolding and budding
they make their way into the light—
awakening
to the rhythms
embedded in the seeds
of lifetimes
born in the star tides
of this universe.
Perhaps as we do.

1992